The People's H.

Images of
South Shields

by

John Carlson & Joyce Carlson

Staff and pupils of South Shields Grammar School. Included are: Pearson, Bage, Todd, Smithson, Slater, Johnson, Crawford, Mr Emerson, Mr Egner, Mr Smith and Perr. Mr Egner the Headmaster was born in Jarrow in 1911. During the Second World War he was a scientific adviser to the RAF. He described himself as a dog man believing animals had very important rights on the Earth. He was Britain's longest serving Headmaster, retiring in 1976.

Previous page: The civic welcome of the Lord Bishop of Durham on 16th June 1921. The parade is just outside of the Town Hall and moving down Fowler Street.

Copyright © John Carlson and Joyce Carlson 1999

First published in 1999 by

The People's History Ltd
Suite 1
Byron House
Seaham Grange Business Park
Seaham
Co. Durham
SR7 0PY

ISBN 1 902527 24 0

Contents

Entertainer Frankie Vaughan on piano, one of the judges in a National Association of Boys' Clubs talent competition. Tommy Duffy, stage name Alan Fox, is in front of the acrobat. Frankie gave a great deal of his time to the Association and visited the Marsden Miners' Hall in October 1955.

Boldon Lane, late summer 1961.

Introduction

This book is the third in a loosely linked series on South Shields, *South Shields Voices* and *The People's History: South Shields* being the other two. None of these books, individually or collectively, are intended to represent a complete history of the town. They are a set of scrap books whose contents have been chosen on interest value to a slowly widening group of people.

When beginning work on the first book we looked just at aspects of the town that were of personal interest to us. Then increasingly we came across other individuals with albums or cardboard boxes stuffed with photographs and family histories and these books have developed into collections of collections as much as anything else. Undoubtedly, these people's interests, perspectives and passions, along with our own, are reflected in the material used and no-one is making a big apology if the same subject has been returned to several times.

While compiling these books two points did emerge. A full history of the town in the twentieth century deserves to be written. Since 1900 Shields seems to have had almost everything except an airport and a proper chronicle of this development, redevelopment and regeneration would be an asset to the borough in the new millennium. Secondly, there are scant photographic records of some areas of the town. With privatisations and amalgamations, the records of many public institutions have been shunted around, re-filed and then lost, while 'newer' areas such as Simonside were probably rarely photographed in their more rural pasts. What material that exists is likely to be in private albums, so if you have anything of interest please allow it to be copied for future generations. Once it's gone, it's gone for good.

The text for this book has been culled from everything between official documents and personal memories to the occasional funny story. While in most cases it has been possible to separate near fact from total fiction, often captions for photographs, that came to us with blank backs, have had to be built up through careful consultation with the families concerned. If you are using them as part of your own research please remember that some dates and places are just a 'best guess'.

The images in this book come from a wide variety of sources and copies are often available. If you are looking for old photographs of Shields the best place to start is in the local studies centre in South Tyneside Central Library. Go down the stairs in the reference library and ask for Keith or Doris. Enquiries concerning the existence, copying and use of Shields Gazette Material should be made in the first Instance to Rob Lawson, Editor, The Shields Gazette, Chapter Row.

Beamish Museum's archives also hold a selection of photographs of South Shields, and others categorised as Harton, Tyne Dock and so on. Please note that while the people and institutions listed above will be pleased to help you, not all facilities are on open access so if you are travelling in from outside the borough telephoning first is probably worthwhile. At the time of writing there are also a growing number of sites on the world wide web, including the *Shields Gazette* and Janis Blower's *Cookson Country* page. Most of the other images in this book come from private collections, contactable through the authors.

John Carlson & Joyce Carlson
South Shields, 1999

South Shields Ladies' Circle members. Mrs M. Kooy, Mrs M. Hamilton, Mrs Margaret Pickering, Ann Shepherd and Mrs Olga Dunlop modelling hats in aid of charity at All Saint's Church Hall in Cleadon Village, 1969.

A TOWN AND ITS PEOPLE

*Busy Streets And Quiet Lanes … Villages And Estates … Moments
At Rest And Lines Of Communication … Places Of Work And
Talking Shops … Jets Of Steam And Screeching Whistles …*

Moon Street tram terminus, Mile End Road. Until 1946 high powered and well
upholstered tramcars departed from here for the wide open spaces at the
southern limits of the Corporation's expanding 'empire' – the housing estates
at the top of King George Road. However, here the date is 1943 when the town
would be battling on through air raids, all development halted, its
infrastructure receiving only essential maintenance. Around 1933 an industrial
publication gave a clinical review of the town: 'South Shields, pop 123,000, is
the third largest town on Tyneside and the least within the influence of
Newcastle. It is a town of several different functions. It is (a) a coal mining
town, (b) a seaport, (c) a shipyard town, (d) a dormitory town for Mid-Tyne,
(e) a pleasure city, (f) a coal shipping port, (g) a shopping centre for a
considerable area. Its site on the hilly ground between the river and the sea is
admirable and on the sea side good use has been made of it. The rest of the
town is pitiably squalid containing both old and dilapidated slums and also
immutable rows of decent mean dwellings. Tyne Dock on the extreme west is a
large importing centre for timber, pitch, grain etc. and a large exporting centre
for coal.'

Ocean Road and the Lawe Top headland from the South Marine Park. Much of today's physical geography could have been very different. Around 1850, when the Tyne Commissioners began developing the river there were never realised schemes to open out and extend the Mill Dam gut into the town as a fully fledged dock. Later there were rumours that the gut was ordered filled in by Dean and Chapter of Durham and the City Fathers of Newcastle to protect the city's trade. If such a scheme had gone ahead maybe much of Kepple Street and Fowler Street would have run alongside the dock and would now be undergoing redevelopment by English Estates as rows of quayside flats.

The exterior of J.C. Carruther's toy and joke shop at No 6 Ocean Road. The old Library stands to the immediate right. A small girl can be just seen peering around the corner at the extreme left. She may be an inhabitant of an upstairs flat.

An advertisement for the Ocean Road Cash Drug Store, *circa* 1910.

Advertisements for the British Oriental Depot, Ocean Road, *circa* 1910. A contemporary visitors' guide commenting on the store remarked: 'Having paid a visit to South Shields, you will doubtless wish to take back a few presents for your friends and probably also some memento as a reminder in the days to come of a pleasant holiday. This being so, a note should be made that at the British Oriental Depot in Ocean Road you will find a most varied assortment of interesting articles specially selected by the proprietor to meet the needs of souvenir seeking visitors. The stock comprises local views, Bohemian and other glass, and embraces practically every novelty on the market in Artistic China and Porcelain Ware, Purses, Photo Frames, Trinket sets and other lines too numerous to mention.'

Ocean Road, 1953. A trolleybus has become detached from the overhead wire. If the 'dewirement' was serious one of a number of blue overhead tower vans would appear to carry out repairs on the wire. As the tower was apparently thoroughly insulated from the ground, crews would nip in as soon as a bus was out of the way, complete the work with the 550 volts overhead power still on, and nip out just before the next bus arrived. After the closure of the system the vans were kept for odd jobs – CU 3534 later being sold to the West of England Transport Collection in Exeter.

FOWLER & BROCK

THE GREAT . .
CASH DRAPERS,

LADIES' & CHILDREN'S COMPLETE OUTFITTERS.

House, Hotel and Ship Furnishers
and Bedding Manufacturers.

Our Customers have one of the largest Stocks in the North of England to select from.

LOWEST CASH PRICES.

FOWLER & BROCK,

59, 60, 61 and 62, King Street,
9, 11, 13 & 15, Smithy Street, & Russell Street,

SOUTH SHIELDS.

Telephone 367.
16

Left: Fowler and Brock advertisement, *circa* 1905. Their premises have been described as: 'comprising of no less than four shops, running through from King Street to Smithy Street, besides one in Russell Street. There are spacious show-rooms for millinery, mantles, Ladies' and Children's Outfitting, Furniture, etc. A noteworthy feature, which indicates the go-ahead manner in which Messrs Fowler and Brock conduct their establishment, is the tea rooms in their stores, which were introduced for the convenience of their customers, who can relieve the tedium of shopping by partaking here of a refreshing cup of tea. The extensive workrooms deal separately with Dress and Mantle making, Millinery etc, and there are also Bedding and upholstering works in Smithy Street. The proprietors are complete House, Hotel and Ship Furnishers and claim to hold one of the largest stocks of Drapery Goods in the North of England.'

The many rooms above King Street have often made convenient offices and meeting places for various organisations. Here members of South Shields Social Democratic Party celebrate their first

anniversary in the town with guest Shirley Williams. Also included are Ron Davison (centre) and Margaret Mills. The Shields party first met on 10th June 1981, and was officially recognised in January 1982. A council seat came when Progressive Party Member for Harton, Greenwell Jewitt, resigned the whip in March 1981 and joined the SDP, becoming its chairman. Two other Progressive Councillors, Ron Davison and Paul Taylor, soon joined him. In spite of the later merger with the Liberals, many South Shields members remained with the continuing SDP.

The exterior of Binns department store. When the Metro finally arrived in South Shields, after much uncertainty and delay, King Street seemed to thrive for a period of time. Possibly people from Hebburn

and Jarrow began taking advantage of the system to pay a visit to Shields. In spite of the council's efforts to improve the town centre, slowly much of the up market trade began travelling out to Gateshead and Newcastle to shop. Binns, Shields' last department store shut its doors in 1995. Nevertheless, King Street still retains much of its former bustle, although many townspeople feel with the loss of Binns a feeling of 'class' has gone from the town.

BAIN & CO.,

Ophthalmic Opticians and Eyesight Specialists.

The only house in South Shields making eyesight testing and spectacle fitting an entire speciality.

Special features of our business.

Experienced Attention.

Each case receives special attention. No inexperienced assistants allowed to consult upon any case of defective Eyesight.

Unique Feature.

The Rooms are specially arranged for the SOLE purpose of testing the Eyesight and the Fitting of Spectacle and Eye-Glass - - - Frames.

Nature of our Work.

Undivided attention is given to the correction of ALL defects of vision.

WE DO NOTHING ELSE.

Difficult Cases.

Those who have trouble in obtaining glasses to suit them are specially invited to consult us.

We strongly recommend our "Bi-focal" Spectacles, which combine far and near sights in one frame.

Persons suspecting that they have defective Eyesight, or are wearing wrong glasses, may have their sight tested and all advice free of charge.

EYESIGHT TESTING ROOMS,

20a, King Street, SOUTH SHIELDS.

33

An advertisement for Bain and Co Opticians, King Street, *circa* 1905.

A Saturday afternoon in King Street, 1954. During, and previous to this decade, most residents of areas such as Chichester, Laygate, Stanhope Road and the like would have shopped for their everyday goods in their local shops, only venturing into King Street on Saturdays for more expensive special items and occasional purchases of 'brown' goods such as fridges and TVs. At least one person told the authors that before the Second World War they would have considered King Street as being 'to expensive to shop in.' Even in the 1950s, to be known as a regular customer at Binns department store, and particularly its food department, would for some people be an important and necessary sign of their social status.

Left: An advertisement for Frank Revel Ironmongers, *circa* 1905.

King Street, *circa* 1900. Minute examination reveals a host of semi-cryptic signs and hoardings above the streets carrying messages such as 'Lockheart's Dinners, 12 to 2' and 'public benefit good boots'. Previous to this date, King Street had been much more residential in nature and maybe some of the older residents would have then regarded such signs a form of visual pollution.

King Street, *circa* 1975. At this time the roadway would be choked with traffic and pedestrians would tightly weave past each other – occasionally, as someone or something blocked their path, being forced to step into the road then back again. Now seeming as anachronistic as

traffic in King Street was the practice of street photographers thrusting a monkey upon passers by, taking their picture and then attempting to sell them copies. Animal legislation seems to have ended this. Around a decade later King Street would be pedestrianised and the streets would be full of the cries of, 'White sports socks, three pairs a pound!'

The staff of Melias Ltd outside their shop in King Street. At the time of writing the Baker's Oven occupies the site, the stonework of Lloyds Bank is just visible to the left.

The Back Loading Bay of Humphrey and Evans' General Dealers, King Street. The delivery cart is being driven by William Moore. The shop was run by his father-in-law, William Evans and his partner Mr Humphrey.

William and Jennie Moore. Mrs Moore's father was William Evans.

Humphrey and Evans shop as seen from the steps of the old Town Hall, 1886. This is one of the oldest known photographs of the area. King Street stretches out to the left, Melias Ltd is the third building down the street. King Street Railway Bridge is visible at the extreme left.

The Market Square, *circa* 1900. Although there are many photographs of the square showing it in use as a fairground or a meeting place for marchers, of shelters being dug and bombed out buses and buildings being examined, these are probably only a tiny fraction of the events that have taken place there. The buildings around the market and their occupants have always been constantly changing, with new arrivals making their own impression. But for a long time traces of the old inhabitants and their properties always remained for the enquiring eye to spot. A faded sign above an upstairs window here, an old wall there. Unfortunately this 'physical continuity' has been almost completely shattered by the Second World War bombing and subsequent redevelopment. Of these former shop fronts, back rooms and upstairs dwellings very few close up images of exteriors or of well lit interiors seem to remain and today these survive mainly in the memories of older residents.

A Corporation bus parked on the Market Square. The old bomb damaged buildings on the west side have gone and they will soon be replaced by Wouldhave House. From left to right it is possible to see Harton Staithes, the old bonded warehouse and the Alum House. Wouldhave House was hit by an explosion itself in 1981, this time caused by a gas main. Eyewitnesses spoke of, 'a hell of a bang, glass shooting right across the market and rubble lying everywhere.' A postman was seen staggering about, his clothes ripped and his face white. Damage was also caused to Franchies Cafe.

A group of Corporation bus conductors on lay over at the Market Square. David Branch is second from the right and Peter Grimes far right. They are all wearing conductor's badges, although the man to the left has two badges, suggesting he is a conductor/relief driver. They are wearing lighter coats which are standard summer dust jackets, while the conductor to the right is wearing a heavier winter coat.

A postcard of St Hilda's Church and Church Way. The card is postmarked 1924 and addressed to a Mrs E. Hepburn in Portsmouth. The message reads, 'My Dear Eva. I am sending this PC as arranged. It has been pouring here all day. I have received your letter and will reply tomorrow. I hope you will enjoy yourself at the review today. Love and kisses, yours, Jack.'

To mark the centenary of the death of William Wouldhave on 2nd October 1921 a new gravestone was erected by public subscription at St Hilda's Cemetery. Tributes were made by the Mayor, Councillor A.D. Johnson, a floral cross laid by the Rev J. Hudson Barker and the last post sounded by Arthur Laycock of the St Hilda Colliery Band. Along with a number of others Wouldhave's body had been left under the roadway during the widening of Church Way and this ceremony seems to have been a way of saying 'sorry'. It would be interesting to know what the participants would think if they could see the state of the gravestone today.

David Branch (right) and Bob Alexander at the Mill Dam in 1953. Behind, the coal powered ferry *Northumbria* waits at the landing stage casting smoke into the air. Unless the wind was completely in the wrong direction its likely that intending passengers would always know when the ferry was in dock or approaching the landing purely by their sense of smell.

Jenny Branch (right) and Nell Tulloch on the Shields ferry, 1929. Behind them can be glimpsed the clutter of buildings at the back of the Market Square. The ferry is likely to be the *Thomas Richardson* which served on the Tyne between 1906 and 1930.

The River Tyne near Tyne Dock Engineering. The twin screw Bergen line mail boat *Venus*, built in 1931 heads out to Norway after departing the Tyne Commission Quay at North Shields. The tug may well be the Lawson-Batey steam tug *Joffre* built 1916.

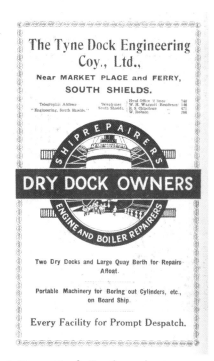

A Tyne Dock Engineering advertisement, *circa* 1930.

Jack Thorp (right) and a workmate at Tyne Dock Engineering around the mid 1950s.

Thrift Street. Although looking very quaint on old photographs many areas of the town would have been cold damp and filthy places to live even until the middle years of this century. Reproduced here is an abridged version of a poem apparently written by a former editor of the *Shields Gazette* around 1860 as he departed the town on a ship bound for London.

Farewell to Shields, the filthiest place,
On old Northumbria's dirty face,
The coal-hole of the British Nation
The fag end of the whole of creation,
The jakes of Newcastle-upon-Tyne,
The banquet-house of dogs and swine,
The paradise of dogs and fleas,
And Human vermin worse than these;
A mass of houses – not a town,
On heaps of cinders squatted down,
Close to the river's cosy edge,
Like moulting hens behind a hedge;
Huge ballast hills, from London brought,
And here like church yard rubbish shot,
Half-clad with scurvy blighted green,
Alone diversify the scene.

Steam tugs whose smoke beclouds the river;
Chimneys forth vomiting for ever,
All sorts of gas to taint the air,
And drive the farmers to despair,
Lighting the corn, the quickset blasting,
And all their prospects overcasting,
Fore scarcely even a weed will blow,
For miles around no trees will grow.

In stunted copse or rugged fence,
Within their baleful influence,
Streets if the name can be applied,
To dingy lanes not ten feet wide,
Bordered by wretched tenements,
Let to poor devils at high rents,
Houses on Dean and Chapter land,
Which if not close packed would not stand.

As for the so called vulgar rabble,
One learns their status from their gabble,
They can't be said to speak at all,
But jabber, croak, grunt and drawl,
'Tis neither English, Scots or Norse,
Though it partakes of all and worse,
If brutes have soles as some pretend,
And after death to Hades wend,
And learn to speak I do expect,
Twill be the Shields dialect,
Farewell to Shields! I shout again,
A long and glad farewell! Amen!
I never liked the place nor did,
The place like me: but god forbid,
I should bear witness false against it;
I have writ truth and hear attend it.

Harry Wray, a mobile crane driver for the Tyne Dock Engineering Company from 1945 to 1969. This photograph was taken at the home of close friend and South Shields Motor Boat Club colleague, Pat Cullen, during Christmas time, *circa* 1970. During his life, Harry had played leading roles in the Club and the Volunteer Life Brigade. He was also a prolific poet and composed principally on local themes. Reproduced below is one of his works:

The Coaly Tyne

Father Thames his name has made
The cradle of colonial trade
The Mersey pioneered the mail
And packet boats in days of sail
The Clyde of clipper building fame
Launched peerless vessels o'er the main
With ships from Wear and Aberdeen
Racing level in the scene.

They each and all have played their part
Perfecting man's most famous art
Since Britain first put out to sea
In skin of goat, and hollowed tree
Which placed this Island in the van
Of Nations, since that day began.

Thro' the centre scene of England's fame
Runs the coaly Tyne of honoured name
For robbed of power, light and heat
London's heart would cease to beat.

To every day on every tide
Viewed afloat from waterside
Are collier ships found out to sea
For England's principality.

The Port-o-Tyne's historic frame
Linked in London's greatest name
With fields of coal explored and mined
Progressively since Roman times
And carried down the shipping lane
Tyne to London once again.

Harry Wray, 1905-1978.

BRIGHAM & COWAN, LTD.,

New Dry Dock 400-ft. by 72-ft. by 24-ft. depth on Sill.

Deep Water Quay, 700-ft. in length.

Telegrams: "DOCKING."
Telephone: P.O., 12; National, 110 & 160.

SOUTH SHIELDS.

FIVE MINUTES WALK FROM SOUTH SHIELDS RAILWAY STATION.

Ship, Boiler, and Machinery Repairs of every description executed with despatch.

Portable Steam and Electrical Machinery for boring out cylinders, piston valve chambers, and drilling out fractured crank pins, furnaces, etc.

A Brigham and Cowan advertisement, 1907. If the complex arrangement of buildings around Thrift Street had survived to this day they would doubtless now be a tourist attraction. However, a series of reports on the area from the early 1800s by the equivalent of local councillors gives some insight into its flavour:

'The road leading to the Alum-House-Ham, close to the North Pillar of the Steam ferry Company's Gates, is in a most dangerous state for Horses, Carts and Carriages, and the landing itself is greatly out of repair. That the whole ought to be taken up reduced and repaved by the Commissioners under the South Shields Improvement Act, within three months … that there are some Boats, large Stones and other articles, lying in the Public Landing

Place at the head of the Long Row, which greatly impede and endanger the Carriage of Goods to and from the River Tyne … that there still exists Nuisance at the corner of Mr Bambridge's Premises in Wapping Street … that there are many Steps projecting from the Houses into the King's Highway, particularly in Wapping and Shadwell Streets, which are encroachments dangerous to Passengers and ought to be removed.'

Left: Mrs Wilkinson, great, great, great, grandmother of Joyce Carlson. The image is taken from a glass negative, *circa* 1855. She is wearing clothes of the extremely modest style favoured by Victoria.

A series of photographs of workers at the Vidor Batteries factory in River Drive. The names are unknown. The images were taken from a set of negatives recovered by postman Dennis Boad from a skip in Oysten Street.

Steam and smoke in South Shields Station Yard. The view is from the ballast hills just below the present Cookson House. The engine to the left (No 7323) may be drawing passenger stock into the station ready for a train to Sunderland. It carries LNER lettering while the locomotive on the right is lettered BRITISH RAILWAYS suggesting this is shortly after nationalisation. At this time the air would be full of the sound of whistles and pounding machinery and the streets marked out by endless arrays of grey slate roofs.

An electric multiple unit lies in the station yard. On the river behind a tug also waits. Towering above them both are the cranes of Brigham and Cowan's.

South Shields Station staff, *circa* 1925. The occasion is likely to be the retirement of the serving station master. Since her own retirement from the station in the late 1970s, ex-bookings clerk Masie Bell has written about her working day.

It's six twenty five am
A queue awaits me.
I hurriedly unlock the door
Of the booking office.
Quickly I put off the alarm.
What's that? Oh it's the cat
Hungry after a night out.
I throw open the little window
'Ha'way bonny lass'
Some one calls.
My day has begun
'First please'
I deal with the workmen
Going up river to the shipyards.
'Two tickets to Jarrow please'
'Ta flower'
'A ticket to Heaven'
Thank goodness I understand
'Pela Miss.'
Day Returns to date
Here's a man with a basket of pigeons
Hurry, hurry I tell myself.
At last the crowd lessens
And with a whistle
A wave from the guard
The six thirty eight chuffs on its way.
What next?
'A return to Torquay please'
'When are you going?
When are you coming back?'
Seats to reserve

'Please Miss can I have two facing the engine'
I dial seats Newcastle
'Second class and non-smoking' I enquire
'No, no I like my baccy'
He continues to talk about
The delights of smoking
A pipe using Condor Twist.
Though sometimes he uses snuff.
Mission accomplished.
I put on the kettle
Grab a sandwich.
I give a sigh and take a balance
Both phones are ringing
The outside and the internal
How can I think
With all this noise?
The outside phone stops ringing
I answer the internal
A telegram – oh my!
Engineering operations – lost property
Railcards to issue – sleepers to book
Refunds to prepare – machine to check
Letters to answer – let's have a look.
Stop for a moment to feed the cat.
Well here's a shipload
Of sailors on warrants
Joining ships or going home.
Head down for a while
At last here's my relief.
Home for a cup of tea
And forty winks.

Russell Street Post Office, *circa* 1905. While this was only one of a chronological series of buildings occupied by the post office in the town, this 1890 structure appears to have been the first designed and built for that purpose. It was opened on 7th July 1890 by Mr J.C. Lamb, one of the permanent secretaries of the GPO and a native of South Shields. As well as counter and sorting facilities the building also contained the town's telephone exchange. The stub of road to the right is Kepple Street much later to be widened and extended under the railway line to Fowler Street, the removed earth becoming part of the support for the extension of the promenade to Trow Rocks.

C. COSSEY,

SADDLER and HARNESS MAKER,

Manufacturer of Trunks and Travelling Bags.

HAND-SEWN HARNESS A SPECIALITY.

5, Russell Street, SOUTH SHIELDS.

Repairs of every Description Neatly Executed.

40

C. Cossey, Saddler, *circa* 1905.

An officer uses a Police Telephone Box in Woodbine Street to communicate with Kepple Street Police Station. As well as these smaller boxes, Shields Police also employed a series of larger ones bearing a passing resemblance to the more famous London Police Boxes and contained medical kit as well as a phone. Apparently if a suspect became violent it was not unknown for an officer to bundle them inside and stand outside holding the door shut with one hand while blowing his whistle and waiting for help to arrive.

Constable Barry King in the old control room in Kepple Street Station, 1958.

Station Road, *circa* 1889. A horse tram is ascending towards Laygate. Its passengers appear 'dressed' – they may be returning from church or a day at the beach but either way they are likely to be some of the town's more 'well to do'. Normally open sided cars only worked as far as Laygate Lane, not through Templetown to Tyne Dock. Horse tram drivers received 22s for 105 hours work, conductors 15s for the same time. Sandboxes to help tackle gradients like Station Road were fitted to the trams and a former passenger once reminisced of seeing a boy conductor empty one over the driver's head. Wielding the horse's whip, the driver then chased the boy round and round in circles until they both became exhausted while passengers shouted, 'We'll be late.'

The demolition of St Hilda Colliery chimney on Saturday 2nd October 1954 seen from Station Road. The chimney, 154 ft tall and containing an estimated 400 tons of brick and stonework was constructed by the Harton Coal Company around 1874. The base was around two and a half feet thick. It appears the chimney was largely redundant by the 1930s and St Hilda Colliery had effectively shut by the beginning of the Second World War. Demolition of the chimney was undertaken by two steeplejacks who hammered out a section of the base. The operation took eight hours longer than expected with hammering continuing until suddenly the men were seen running quickly away from the stack. It fell around a minute later. Reportedly after the demolition, a hammer lost down the chimney by a worker involved in its construction was found and returned by the NCB to his grandchildren in Australia.

Muriel Hanson (née Gardener), thirteen years of age, a resident of Commercial Road in the High Shields area, 1944. Muriel recalls: 'We had some happy times around Commercial Road. My brother was ten years older than me and had to look after me. He used to take me all over with him and he used to get sick of me. I've got a mark on the top of my brow because he used to hump me up over his shoulder to carry me and one day I went right over the top and fell head first to the ground in front of him.

Next to the Pavilion, opposite the Lord Clyde pub, there was a billiard hall where he used to play cards. One day, for some reason, he suddenly jumped up, rushed out and left me. I was taken to the Police Station and my mother had to pay sixpence to get me out.

I used to be friendly with my Uncle Kit who used to have the Phoenix public house in Laygate Lane and with his daughter who was the same age as me. We used to go down into the cellars  during the air raids and sleep on chair beds. Kit's mother, my grandmother, used to live down Palmerston Street opposite the Zion Hall and she used to scrub the bar out to get her gill of beer.

My Uncle Joe was a publican at the Brunswick in Laygate Lane. When his wife Barbara was hard up she would pawn his shirts at Oranges at the top of Green Street. When she wanted his white shirt for work she would have to go along to the shop. Often she didn't have any money so she would say she had forgotten the number of the ticket. Then she would spot a white shirt, usually someone else's, but point to a parcel on a different shelf, and one that was always high up, and say is that it up there? Then, when the man got a pair of steps to climb up to get it, she would sneak the one out of the other parcel and take it home so Joe could go to work.

Isaac 'Bert' Wilkinson and his wife Elizabeth (left) with Sarah and Frank Raine. Bert and Elizabeth were residents of Bewick Street and ran the Troubadours Concert Party. Bert and Frank met in the DLI during the First World War. In France, aged seventeen, they were chased through a wood by German soldiers. Bert escaped with two bullet wounds in the arm, but Frank was taken prisoner and sent to the salt mines where ill treatment disabled him permanently. All on the photograph were actually teetotallers.

Sheila Bruce (centre) and her friends Ruby (right) and Sylvia Fraser (left) in the lane at the back of the family house in Lyton Street, 1938.

Demolition of some of the rows of former shops and houses in the Frederick Street area, *circa* 1981. Much of this area is now occupied by a dual carriage way.

E. H. GRAY, Frederick Street Dairy,
6, FREDERICK STREET, SOUTH SHIELDS.

Teas and Refreshments provided at moderate charges.
New Milk, Fresh-Laid Eggs, Finest Dairy Butter. All local produce.
Parties Catered for on the shortest notice. *Telephone 1 Y.*

An advertisement for E.H. Gray, *circa* 1910.

Joyce Dryden in Brownlow Road, *circa* 1948.

An illuminated scroll presented to the family of Henry Emmerson, a joiner in his twenties from South Palmerston Street who was killed shortly after arriving in Belgium during the First World war. Enemy soldiers tunnelled under the hill where he was stationed and set off an explosive charge that killed him and many of his comrades. He left a wife, Martha, and three daughters, Esther, Martha and Lillian. His wife refused to believe he was dead such a short time after departing these shores and kept his coat hanging behind the kitchen door ready for when he came back. Finally, a friend who had enlisted at the same time and was there at the time of the explosion came home on leave, told her what had happened and a short time afterwards the coat came down off the door.

From left to right: Beryl, Marjorie and Lily Knock in the Candlish Street area, 1943.

Hilda Branch, 14 years of age, in 1917.

Isabel Oliver (right) and Barbara Watson in a back lane of Dean Road, 1945.

Jean, Rita and Phylis. A portrait taken in Hamilton Studios, Ocean Road

Gannie Clements. Her granddaughter, Sheila Bruce, remembers how like many old people of the 1930s she was given residence in the attic of the family home, in this case Lyton Street.

Emily Charlotte Bruce with the master's dog when she was in service.

Female members of the Bruce family pose as bridesmaids, *circa* 1925.

The Todd family, Ethel, May, Nancy and Jim in John Williamson Street, *circa* 1917.

Left to right: Bobby Lofthouse, Chris Johnson and Tommy Best in the back lane of Francis Street, 1937. A Walls' 'Stop me and buy one' ice cream seller stands behind them.

Two photographs of Ernie Branch in the back yard of his parent's house in the Francis Street area, *circa* 1924.

Holborn, *circa* 1981. A scrap yard stands on the site once occupied by the Corporation Power Station. Harton High Staithes stood alongside until they were closed in 1977. A flint glass works also occupied the site to the rear of the scrapyard. Although the view is undoubtedly a mess, it would gladden the heart of any model railway enthusiast looking to add a bit of atmosphere to his layout.

The Middle Docks, *circa* 1981. In April 1976 Tony Benn visited the docks with his wife Caroline who named the first British owned and designed drill ship, the 15,000 ton *Dalkeith*. He was less than warmly received by a group of the town's Young Conservatives protesting against the Labour government of the day.

The Neptune Inn and Burton's Cellars in Corstophine Town. This area later became part of Edwards Dock. A document relating to the 'London Hotel' reads: 'I JAMES HENDERSON, being the license holder of the 'LONDON HOTEL' Corstorphine Town, South Shields do hereby undertake that intoxicating liquors shall be sold in the snug or family department of such licensed premises for consumption off the premises only, and no intoxicating liquor sold in this department shall be consumed on the premises at any time from and after this date. 30th day of June 1910.'

Readhead's Offices and the Cookson's Arms public house, 1939

Harton Junction, Tyne Dock. Today's Metro runs to the left following the 1872 line to Newcastle. Boldon Lane runs from left to right under the tracks in the mid ground. From around 1870 to 1935 this area could be described as

the town's throat with almost all passenger traffic and freight from the Harton Coal Company Collieries, High Shields good depot and the riverside foundries and yards passing through. The houses to the left housed railway workers, in the distance stands the 1883 Tyne Dock Station and the former Deans Estate. Wright's Biscuit factory is to the right.

The 1859 Tyne Dock Station building. The metal fence to the front is the ramp up from Boldon Lane into the 1883 station – now it runs into the forecourt of the 1984 Metro Station. Boldon Lane originally ran to the right of the picture, level with the railway but was diverted under the line around 1883. The 1859 building was demolished in stages, the section on the left going last in the mid 1980s.

A trolleybus passes the Boldon Lane entrance to Tyne Dock Station in 1959. The bus will be waiting to pick up passengers from the connecting train from Newcastle. Although most of the structures here survive today, this area once seemed so much darker and gloomier and the heavy iron gates lend an almost gothic note to the view.

North Eastern Railway locomotive driver Sidney Eastwood (centre) at Green Lane sheds.

The Ashley Road area, 1922. George Frederick Auld and Foster Bainbridge playing on a patch of ground. Note the chicken to the left.

The entrance to Tyne Dock, looking down Hudson Street, *circa* 1900. To the right is the old Dock Hotel. The large building to the left is a grain warehouse. It was demolished in 1964.

The *Broadhurst* in Tyne Dock. One of the dock's famous coal staithes is visible to the right.

Two groups of people in the Ashley road area. *Above*: A longhand caption on the back says, 'Here we are again. Do you recognise Madge? She has had her hair bobbed now around six weeks ago.' *Below*: A group of young boys. The caption on the back reads 'The back lane boys. Fred Auld, Bobby Glendening (Canada), dear little Jim.'

Staff of Harton Dye Works. The date is unknown although it is likely to be the 1920s. Moor Lane is to the right. At the turn of the century men received 20s for a week of around 56 hours, women 14s.

Inside Harton Dye Works, 1956. Included are: Maureen Tate, Marion Ridge, Violet Branch and Evelyn Taylor.

Staff of Harton Dye Works at a Christmas dance in 1947.

A Christmas dance at the Majestic Ballroom for Harton Dye Works staff, 1957.

HARTON. (1150.)

Harton Village around 1912 with the Ship Inn centre. Although telephone poles intrude on to the streets, a telephone connection would be beyond the financial grasp of most people. It would be interesting to know the dynamics and tensions unfolding in the village at the time. Its council would be resisting the advances of that of South Shields and seeking solicitors' advice over the activities of the Tyne Improvement Commission. On incorporation the village was divided up into several council wards. How far the new boundaries were drawn up for political reasons is unclear, but the houses to the right became part of the Westoe ward. Unusual in Shields in that it contains almost no council houses, it only recently fell to Labour in local elections.

Construction of private housing in Mitchell Gardens. Previously the site of post-war prefabricated housing, the area lay derelict and overgrown for many years and was often used by residents to exercise dogs and stage  bonfires on Guy Fawkes' Night. Children also made use of it as an adventure playground. One favourite activity involved pouring paraffin down the abandoned drainage system, throwing in a lighted match and watching the sinks in the road blow out.

Harton Village shops, *circa* 1955. Except for the removal of the trees and the addition of a car park and some new shop fronts, the view is little changed today.

A picturesque vista of Linden Gardens, *circa* 1912. While many of the photographs of Harton Village from around this time give an impression of a very rural agricultural community it's clear from this postcard view that there was also a wealthy, residential area.

A horse drawn omnibus on Sunderland Road, Harton. At one point a service departed every twenty minutes from the village for Shields, operated by the town's Horse Tramway Company. This seems to be the south side of the village so where exactly the service terminated is unclear. Fares on the Westoe omnibus were collected on the trust system, passengers dropping coins into a brass box as they alighted. The driver would listen out for the sound of coins and would often glare down suspiciously through a hole in the roof at those about to alight. Apparently so well known was this practice that a company of travelling actors produced a skit 'The Westoe Omnibus' which involved a group of passengers being too frightened to get off the bus.

Holder House Farm, *circa* 1900. The man standing on the corn binder is Thomas Young. This area later became the Holder House Estate.

The New Ship Inn. In spite of its popularity the authors have been able to find out very little about this pub and why it was (presumably) named in relation to the Old Ship Inn, Cleadon. Controversy was generated when a conservatory was added to the front of the building, local residents apparently protesting, 'It will be lager louts next!'

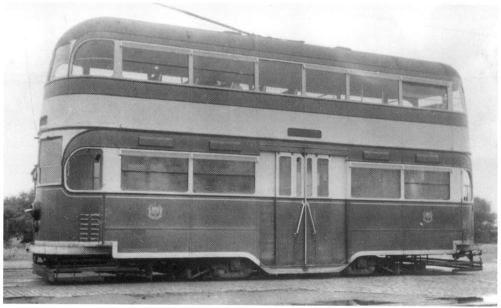

Tramcar No 52 at the Ridgeway, shortly before the outbreak of the Second World War. During the 1930s this area would be almost a foreign land to many Shields people. In the years around the Second World War cameras and film were often restricted in supply and as with many of the other images contained in this book, this photograph was taken with a box brownie and a certain amount of family negotiation. 'Awe go on dad, take that one.' In this case it was at the behest of a young transport enthusiast, David Packer, who went on to photograph many of the transport systems in the region.

Three photographs of the Branch family taken on the Cleadon Park estate in the 1920s. *Top left*: George Branch and his son Ernie in Park Avenue. *Above*: Ernie Branch on his bike aged two in 1924. *Left*: Six of the seven Branch sisters, Hilda, Nell, Jenny, Mary, Molly and Maggie. The tenants viewed themselves as privileged to live on the estate. It was almost a village on its own, the surrounding fields were full of cows munching grass and mooing could be heard through open windows. The streets seemed wide and empty, only one resident was a private car owner. Gardens were kept immaculate and full of flowers and vegetables. Although the estate was officially part of the slum clearance programme, rents were relatively high and priority was often given to former servicemen. It seems few people from the worst areas in 'Old Shields' made it on to the estate.

A trolleybus passing the Marsden estate in 1959. As the King George Road tramcars were linked with the development of the Cleadon Park estate this trolleybus route allowed housing to develop around Marsden even further from the beaten track.

Albert and Catherine Wilkinson, residents of Marsden, with their son Raymond. Catherine once served as a councillor for the Horsley Hill ward and both were well known as the proprietors of the very popular fish and chip shop in Moffet Street which even attracted customers from Cleadon and outlying districts.

Marsden Cottage Station, formally Salmon's Hall, on the 'Marsden Rattler' line to Whitburn. The authors do not know the name of the gentleman standing on the platform. Passengers were carried on the route from around 1885. Until the construction of the Coast Road and the estates around Horsley Hill, this area would have been relatively isolated from the town, with even the train service only running in as far as Westoe Lane. Some excitement came to this area on the night of 8th August 1916 when a Zeppelin apparently making for the nearby Frenchman's Fort dropped bombs around Salmon's Hall. Although a horse appears to have been the sole casualty, many local residents in their night-clothes fled across the fields to the shelter of the caves under Marsden Cliffs.

From left to right: George Hodgson, Ken Brew, David Branch, Stewart Davidson, Brian Smith and Herbert McLachlan on the cliffs overlooking Marsden Bay, 1956.

Horsley Hill Farm. As Shields grew the farm was gradually surrounded by new estates – with St Cuthbert's Avenue and Frenchman's Way from the south and Sheldon and Southfield Roads from the north. It's likely that Cheviot Road now runs almost smack through the centre of what was the pond.

The Horsley Hill public house at Horsley Hill Square. This area was one of the last housing developments built in what were wide open spaces. In the 1980s there were plans to hold a Sunday market in the car park of the public house.

Trolleybus driver and Horsley Hill resident, Stan Walsh.

SUNDERLAND ROAD, WESTOE, SO SHIELDS.
5005.G.H.N/C.

Westoe Village, *circa* 1910. Sunderland Road leads off to the right, Imeary Street to the left. The Ingham Infirmary is visible to the back. Superficially the layout is similar to that of today, but the importance of the streets has changed. The far end of the recently constructed Imeary Street would not run smoothly under Westoe Bridges but swung sharp right to run alongside the Harton Coal Company's lines and then on to Westoe Road. The electric tram line, which passed the Town Hall on its way to Westoe, and the horse trough to the left are almost symbolic markings out of the battleline in a dispute between two councils and two different ways of life. The length of track seen here is running close to the borough's boundary with the parish of Harton. A set of points are just visible in the foreground curving off to the right, then abruptly stopping. They would have been laid in anticipation of building a light railway extension through Harton towards Sunderland. However, this was something the Corporation would refuse to do until the parish became a part of Shields, a move strongly opposed by the parish council. As parish councillors approached Westoe in the motor bus service provided by the North Eastern Railway Company, the road beneath their wheels would change from a rough surface to carefully laid sets and cobbles. The sight of the points sweeping out to meet them would surely have been an ominous sign of things to come.

Pratt's Wine and Spirits Building at the corner of Dean Road and Imeary Street, Westoe. The date is around 1900. Pratt's had previously worked from premises in Holborn. This new building was constructed around 1883 on the site of Wallis or 'Hannah Stokes' Cottages which also stood across what is now the top of Imeary Street.

Westoe Village looking east. Apart from the addition of double yellow lines there have been few visual changes here. However, one of the buildings towards the right was completely demolished and then rebuilt in the 1980s.

A long team of horses pulling a heavy casting pause near Westoe in their journey from South Shields to Sunderland. The building behind is now the site of The County public house. It would be interesting to know why this load is making what must have been a fairly difficult journey by road instead of being sent via the North Eastern Railway.

The widening of Sunderland Road, 1922. The County pub is visible in the centre. By this time South Shields Council is in charge of Harton. The ground to the right is being laid out as the Readhead Park. Amongst Harton Parish Council's arguments against incorporation in the borough had been that its parks were too far at the other end of the town to be of use to village residents who would nevertheless be paying rates to support them. Perhaps the Readhead Park was seen as a means of proving them wrong after the fact.

Right: Eddie Angel aged four in 1935.

Eddie recalls: 'I left Mortimer Road School when I was fourteen, just as the long summer holidays started. I was disappointed because as the other kids were enjoying themselves, I was starting work for fourteen bob a week as an errand boy at Duncan's the grocers on Stanhope Road. I was boening bacon, cleaning brasses, sweeping sawdust off the floor, cleaning the massive windows and pushing a barrow full of groceries around to customers' houses. My father thought I wasn't getting enough money and got me a job on the tugs. I was out all hours of the night and day for two pounds ten shillings a week. A taxi would come to pick us up, but if we slept in it wouldn't wait, so we would have to walk down to Brigham's in the freezing cold dark. After that I worked in Sharp's shoe factory cutting out soles and heels on a big press. I was always cutting my wrists on the skiving machine that trimmed the sole. Once I was chatting to this lass and accidentally shaved off part of my thumb.

My mother had to go into hospital because she had tuberculosis and eventually she was sent to Poole Sanatorium for an operation. She was very upset because she had never been away from Shields. On the day of the operation I was working in Woodhouse's furniture store in King Street and one of the lads came into the basement and said, "Ted, there is a woman wants to see you upstairs."

So I put a white dust coat on, went upstairs and it was my mother. I said, "Mother what the hell are you doing here?"

She said, "I've come home to die son." I was shocked to hell. She had refused the operation. They told her she had a fortnight to live, and off she had gone to Shields. She lasted another twenty years and sadly everyone else who had that operation, bar one, died because of it.

Then I worked in Wigg's record department with Miss Johnston. I couldn't play a note but I was expected to sell musical instruments. So when a customer would come in to buy a piano, I would tell them, "This one is a lovely model." I would lift the lid, pose my hands as if ready to play, then exclaim, "What am I doing? I know the tone is good, but I am not the one who is going to play it. You sit down here." It worked every time and I sold loads of pianos without playing a note.'

The Town Council and Officials on the Town Hall steps during Mayor's Sunday, November 1926. Over the years the new Town Hall's chambers and corridors have seen a number of intellectual, political and physical struggles over the direction of council policy. Yet many of its former leading lights seem to have faded into the gloom. Here the gentleman in the 'wig' is Mr J. Moore Hayton. He was only the third town clerk appointed, beginning his service in 1892. He piloted bills through parliament in 1896, 1900, 1903 and 1921 and saw the introduction of electric light, electric trams, the town abattoir, seaside improvements, the widening of Mile End Road, Ocean Road, Church Way, Laygate Lane and the construction of King George Road. In the ornate uniform and medals is Police Chief Constable William Scott. He was appointed in 1902 and died in 1928, shortly after this picture was taken. His funeral cortege was over a mile long and watched by thousands as it made its way from his house in Belgrave Terrace to St Michael's Church and then to Harton Cemetery.

A group of councillors and officials inside the new Town Hall extension. Included are: Albert Elliott, Robert Scott, Mrs Raffle, Elizabeth Diamond and Lilian Jordison.

Gladys Rodgers. Her mother, Ada, ran the gown shop opposite the Town Hall. The shop's motto was, 'Where the wise shop' under a symbol of an Owl.

An unknown Shields woman from a 'Speed Photography' of Ocean Road. This style of dress marked out the better off in the 1930s and in updated form was still common in many of the town's 'better off' areas until the 1970s.

Billy, Bob, Lizzie, and their mother Mary Lamb, 1951. They lived in a flat above Carter's the Chemist in Fowler Street and are pictured here in their back lane. Several years later Mary's brother, William, fell asleep on their settee while smoking and  his lighted cigarette set fire to the building. After the fire his body was found in the remains of the chemist's shop still lying on the settee where it had crashed through the burning ceiling.

MILLER & CO.,

High-Class GROCERY & PROVISION MERCHANTS.

English and Continental Produce.   French and Italian Goods in great
variety.   Established Half a Century.

**Government and Hotel Contractors. The Largest and most
Up=to=Date Grocery Establishment in the Provinces.**

34 and 36,
FOWLER STREET, **SOUTH SHIELDS.**
Deliveries by own Covered Vans daily.

Above and opposite: Advertisements for Miller and Douglas' shop on the
corner of Fowler Street and Kepple Street from around 1910. The first
thing former customers seem to remember of the inside is the strong
smell of coffee. Note the empty ground to the left.

Above: A tramcar loads up at the bottom of Fowler Street. For many years this area was lined with queues of people waiting for transport to various parts of the borough. Late at night, as the cinemas turned out, this area could suddenly become a mass of happy jostling people packing themselves into trams and buses which would labour up Fowler Street and then begin dispensing their loads just after the Town Hall. This photograph was taken by Dr Nicol, one of a few transport enthusiasts actively photographing British systems in the 1920s. He travelled with his attractive Italian wife who was apparently a keen amateur tram driver herself. When they visited a depot he would ask if a car could be brought out to be photographed and then she would ask if she could drive it out.

An international group of students in Ocean Road, 1995. Included are: Shirley Mei Jung Huang and Giuseppe Baffi. A contemporary guide to the town posted on the internet described Shields' nightlife as, 'Second only to Newcastle in the North East – it's loud and there's much of it. From the Metro Station the bright lights of Ocean Road and its numerous drinking palaces tempt the visitor. A top pub crawl starts up by the Town Hall with a swift pint of 80 bob in the Britannia. Next door is Oscar's and then move down to the Voyager on Anderson Street via the Bowler Hat, a club so small a couple of fat men tend to make it look packed. After that get on to Ocean Road and Dexter's, Raffle's, Roxanne's, the Bizz Bar, the 69 Club, Kirkpatrick's, the Criterion and the Ship and Royal. A pint of Theakstons in the Scotia, or a quick Stones in the Stag's Head and then get into Idol's followed by the Venue, an ex-cinema and now 'super pub'. Finally, Oz is the top nightclub in Shields. The more discerning drinker might head for the riverside – the Alum House is by the ferry landing and usually does six or so real ales. The Steamboat and Rose and Crown are next to the docks and also do a canny pint. No trip to Shields is complete without going to the Grotto – a pub built into the cliff at Marsden Bay. Otherwise, head for the Bamburgh or the Sundial on the sea front. Finally, if you want to see naked women dance in cages go to the Brunswick on Laygate Lane. If you don't, don't.'

SCHOOLDAYS

*The Grammar School ... Cleadon Park Infants ... Laygate Lane
School ... Stanhope School ... St Gregory's ... Harton
Comprehensive ...*

Pupils of South Shields Grammar Technical School for Boys, 1956.

Laygate Lane School, *circa* 1927. Ernie Branch is third from the right in the front row. One of the teachers is Miss Scrubb.

Laygate Lane School, *circa* 1927. Lily Eastwood is third from the left in the second row. Sidney Eastwood is in the centre of the front row.

Pupils of Laygate Lane School, 1949.

Construction of the new building for Laygate Lane School and demolition of the old one in 1971.

Stages in the demolition of the old Laygate Lane School building in 1971. Although newer school buildings are almost always better suited to the needs of young children, something of the character is often lost when the old ones are demolished.

Baring Street School, 1932. The headmistress, Miss Starling, is on the left and the teacher is Miss Crane. Before the Second World War female teachers were not allowed to marry unless they gave up their job but as male teachers were called up for the forces the shortage of teachers meant that regulation was waved. Included in the back row are: Janet Coult, Jean Forest, Agnes Gudgson Edith Gollop, Margaret White, Margaret Burn. In the second row are: Margaret Stephenson, Elsie James. In the third row are: Hilda Chappell, Mary Smith, Betty Moore, Isabelle Harle, Margaret Wood. In the front row are: Jean Atkinson, Jenny Robson, Violet Anderson, Jean Laing, Margaret Coverdale and Emma Wraith.

Empire Day at Baring Street School, 1933. Left to right: Jean Atkinson, Elsie Scott, Isabel Harle, Marjorie Mee and Elsie Manning. The cardboard lamb visible was an advert for New Zealand Lamb.

South Shields Grammar School for Girls, Iolanthe Terrace.

Pupils of Westoe County Secondary School, 1948. Included are: Joe
Woodcock, Jack Berry, Tom Elsy, Alan Anderson, Don Rollins, Tom Walker,
Frank Boddy, George Abblett, David Branch, Ken Bullock, Derek Harbron, Joe
James, Bobby Nichol, Terry Mayne, James Turnbull, Billy Hope, Les Chilton,
Alan Kennedy, Les Arkle, Jimmy Melville, Robert Miller and Derek Johnson.

Pupils of Cleadon Park Infants School, 1949. The school building began life as a hut. The 1930s Infants School was ultra modern for its time, featuring grass lawns and a glass covered veranda.

A group of girls from Stanhope Infants School, 1946/7. Included are: Joyce Colden, Joyce Foster, Marjorie Solomon, Brenda Quinn, Pat Martin, Audrey Watling, Joyce Dryden Ann Winter, Sheila Bradlow, Dorothy Kettle, Mary Pargeter, Mavis Hodgeson, Pat Rutter and Muriel Hall.

Mrs Barris' class, Stanhope School, 1948.

Mr Longstaff's class at Stanhope School, 1951.

St John's School in Beach Road after its closure. This is often thought of as one of the better schools in the town, with many of its former pupils going on to well paid jobs, some in the Town Hall just a short distance down the road. The building has since been demolished although some of the stonework was incorporated into a block of flats built on the site.

Pupils of Garth Crescent Infants School, *circa* 1968. The school is situated very near the beach and in the summer pupils would often be collected by their parents and taken for a picnic lunch at Frenchman's Bay.

Pupils of South Shields Grammar Technical School for Boys, 1956 (above) and 1966 (below).

South Shields Grammar School, Form 6I, 1974-75. Included are: Hetherington, Jetha, Whitfield, Hull, Bates, Crawford, Bell, Cragg, Olsen, Huddart, Freeman, Gillespie, Brooks, Edmundson, Emberton, Nicholson, Parker, Hellam, Kirikal, Elliott and Stewart.

South Shields Grammar School/Harton Comprehensive Music group, 1974-75. The school was opened on 16th September 1936 by the then Bishop of Durham, Dr Henson. The building was described as: 'The most important edifice built by the Corporation since the erection of the Town Hall.' The first Headmaster was Mr William Lucas. The building was later extended both upwards and outwards, a process not without some local noise and heartache, and by the 1970s was accommodating around 1,100 pupils and 70 staff. In 1971 the timetable was the first in the country to be drawn up by a computer. Previously it had taken two masters three weeks, now it took a machine in Trondheim, Norway, 16 minutes. On completion it filled the wall of a classroom. When the school became mixed sex in 1979, late completion of building work, including the installation of girls' toilets, delayed the start of the new term and caused some heated debate in the local press.

CHURCH AND SOCIAL

St Andrew's … Westoe Methodist … St Gregory's … St Peter's …
St Lawrence's … St Hilda's …

The Rev Cornelius Cronin, Parish Priest at St Gregory's Church, Sunderland
Road during the celebrations for his Golden Jubilee as a priest in 1976. He was
seventy-five. The Rev Cronin joined the St Gregory's Parish in 1942, when it
was formed out of part of the St Bede's Parish – the parish where he had
previously served as priest.

The original altar for St Gregory's Church was in a room in a private house and was used for daily Mass, Sunday School and Benediction until the church was opened.

Father John Deans, first Parish Priest of St Gregory's, *circa* 1935.

Father Dunlop, Father Cronin and Father Conway outside St Gregory's Church entrance in 1960.

A Garden Party at St Gregory's Church.

An ivy covered St Peter's Church at Harton, *circa* 1935. While researching this book the authors found a curious rhyme called *The King of Harton*. Before becoming very cryptic it begins:

You villagers of Harton
Who frequently have teas
And everytime appear to have
A 'battle and a breeze'.

Your church has been the reason
Of squabble in the place
You fight for who's to take the lead
In this good work of grace.

Members of St Peter's Church, *circa* 1935. Included are: Mr G. Hardy (Warden and Treasurer), Mr Crowell, Archie Henderson, Mr Lamb, Donald Murray, Mr Ashworth (Vicar's son), Tom Staddon (Sexton), Alan Hayden, Alan Masson, Douglas Murray, Cecil Scarf, Alan Edgar, Duncan Murray, Bill Wait, Harry F. Beverley, The Rev G. Ashworth, Sandy Wait, Robert Murray and Alan Burn.

Arthur Archibald Phillpotts of St Peter's Church, 1864-88.

E. Burrows, Curate of St Peter's Church, 1885-87.

W.J. Simm, Curate, 1881-85.

W.C. Carr, Curate, 1887-88.

The Rev Ronald Tucker, who served as the third Minister of Westoe Methodist Church from September 1939 to August 1945.

The Rev Haner.

Members of Westoe Methodist Church. Included are: Annie Young, Hilda Carr, Marjorie Coates, Marion Shaw, Betty Pitchers, Molly Burkett and Minister Leslie G. Holding.

St Andrew's Church Concert Party, 1950. Included are: Edward Short, Colin Robinson, Mavis Russell, Dorothy Tulloch, Jean Legg, Carol Greaves, Joyce Dryden and Ann Short. The church at Talbot Road opened in 1902. It went on to boast a football team that won the South Tyne Alliance League Cup in the 1935-36 season. During the Second World War it was taken over as a first aid post and the congregation was left with only one small room. The church later became the Charles Young Centre.

An Easter bonnet dance performed by members of St Andrew's Church Concert Party, 1950.

The first St Lawrence's Church building in Centenary Avenue. The prefabricated wooden building came originally from Durham where it had been used as a college chapel for St Bede's College. It was given to St Peter's Parish, Harton to be used as a mission church for the then developing area of Horsley Hill and arrived on the Centenary Avenue site in 1939. However, it was one of the first buildings in the town to suffer war damage and didn't actually open its doors for worship until 1941. St Lawrence's was only licensed for weddings in 1972 with Miss Margaret Ann Roberts of Falstone Avenue and Clifford Brock of Boldon Colliery the first couple down the aisle. Rumour has it that the old church was so small the pews had to be shifted apart at weddings to form an aisle, then shifted back at the end of the ceremony.

Construction work underway on the second St Lawrence's building. Plans had been made in the 1960s for the building to be replaced by a larger permanent structure, but unfortunately the shifting seams of Harton Colliery, which was fast approaching the end of its own working life, were disturbing buildings in the Centenary Avenue area. New building work was impossible until the NCB investigated the problem and the congregation soldiered on with their wooden building. In 1984 St Lawrence's split from St Peter's to form its own parish and in 1987 a campaign started to raise £220,000 for a new building. Although much was raised within the parish, considerable help came from outside. Members of St Francis Parish in Solihull raised £5,000, some of them even taking part in a 270 mile sponsored walk to Shields. The old church was demolished in 1990.

Right: Tom Finch, in the back room of his home, constructing a life size statue of the living Christ for the Church of St Lawrence.

The interior of St Hilda's Church, *circa* 1924. A number of buildings stood on the area outside the church until 1862. Included were Eskdale the fishmonger and a wooden hut used as the studio of the Downey Brothers, apparently the town's first photographers.

St Hilda's Choir and Clergy, *circa* 1924. The Vicar is Canon Hudson-Barker.

Laying the foundation stone for St Hilda's Youth Club, Coronation Street.

St Hilda's Church AFC in the 1911-12 season. Included are: J. Clark (committee), J. Riddle, W.J. Swinbanks (captain), G. Taylor, Rev C.T. Parkinson, R. Wanless (committee), R. Pattinson (committee), R. Hall (committee), F. Bewick, Canon Roberson, J.A. Gardner, W. Wanless, W. Chipchase, W. Rutherford, R. Young, (vice-captain), T. Hay, D. Pollard and J. Pattinson.

Medical Mission Sisters singing on the steps of the old Town Hall, 1967.

The blessing of St Oswald's RC Church, 1965.

LET ME
ENTERTAIN YOU

Eddie Angel ... The Alexandra Players ... Alan Fox ... Tom Best ...
Tom Finch ... The Savoy ... Carnivals And Colliery Bands ...
Hospital Radio South Tyneside ...

Tommy Duffy entertaining under his stage name of Alan Fox at the La Strada Club, South Shields. Tom recalls: 'I began singing when I was a kid. I joined Tyne Dock Youth Club, but I was so shy I would stand in the office with the microphone and sing to the members outside in the hall through loudspeakers. Frankie Vaughan came around when we had competitions in the clubs. I was one of the lucky ones to win the north-east heat at the Regent Cinema at Westoe and was invited down to the Royal Festival Hall in London. I was in Readhead's shipyard one day and on stage with Frankie Lane, Vera Lynn, Alma Cogan, Billie Cotton and Ted Loon the next day.

Eddie Angel aged four (left) and as a young bodybuilder (below). Over the years Eddie has starred in both local and national television programmes as well as making regular appearances in theatre. He is also known for his radio commercials, where one of his specialities is his ability to impersonate the voice of Frank Sinatra: 'That's my kind of store, Newmill!' He began learning the acting trade in South Shields: 'I always wanted to be an actor. I got into trouble at school because I would always write my name, Edward Rea – Actor, in my schoolbooks. I started off when I was in the Army in the Far East, then I did a few cruise ships singing Frankie Lane songs and when I came back I did a few clubs. One of the first was Fletcher's in Catherine Street. Then I joined the Northern Studio of Dramatic Art in Roman Road and was taught elocution by a brilliant, wonderful man called Robert Monteagle. He had been the manager and director of the Queen's Theatre. When it came to props Robert could make anything. He made a Roman uniform for an actor, Jack Gallager, with lemonade bottle tops as studs. He made skulls out of papier mashie and stained glass windows out of sack cloth. Later I took to writing letters to Mr Johnston at the *Gazette* and eventually I was offered a job. I was sent to cover a cricket match in Woods Terrace and wrote three sides of foolscap. Anxiously, I waited for the first edition to come out and couldn't find my piece. Then I found three lines on the back page.'

Flo Thorburn in costume as Cinderella at the Alexandra Theatre in Wallis Street, *circa* 1935. Her husband is featured on the following pages.

Frank S. Heywood (*above*), of the Alexandra Players, pictured in a variety of roles: in Princess Caprice (*above right*), as Fagin (*facing page, left*) and Mr Brownlow (*facing page, right*) from Oliver Twist. His daughter Joan recalls: 'The Alexandra Theatre was down Wallace Street beside the Gazette office. The building had been a temperance hall. My mother, Flo Thorburn, and father, Frank Heywood, ran the repertory company, the Alexandra Players for ten years. I spent the first five years of my life around the theatre, it only closed when the area was bombed and its roof was declared dangerous. I think the theatre was run by a woman called Eva Elwes. Once my parents and the rest of the company had gone to the beach and out to sea in a boat and then couldn't get back in again because of the sea swell. They missed curtain up by half an hour. Eva was fuming and as they were about to go on stage she told them, "You'll do this show and no more". They went right through the performance thinking that was it. But after the show was finished Eva realised that she didn't have anyone else so they were all rehired.

The routine was that they would start rehearsing a show for the following week at 11 o'clock on a Tuesday morning until one o'clock. Then in the afternoons and evenings they would perform that week's show. Then the next week they would perform the show they had been rehearsing and start rehearsing another one. They also did two weeks pantomime every year.

In the orchestra pit were Ethel Stitt, a photographer from Ocean Road who played the violin and Ernie Ekin who played the piano. Stella Sheriff was there with her dancing girls. Once they were playing angels dancing around while my mother lay dying. She looked up and they were all crying and the mascara was running down their faces. It looked quite funny. Sometimes the audience would get caught up in the show. Once when mum was playing Maria Martin in *Murder in the Red Barn* in a scene were she was walking across a field in the dark, someone shouted out, "Look out, the bugger's behind you."

The theatre would smell of oranges. The audience were always eating fruit and peas pudding sandwiches. Sometimes the players would look down at the audience and see a woman breast feeding her baby. Then the baby would fall asleep and the woman would be so absorbed in the play she would forget to do herself back up.

The theatre cat had full run of the theatre and would often stroll on to the stage if there was a fireside scene on and sit on the mat.'

Thomas Duffy (Alan Fox) presenting an electric clock to Brenda Green and Billy Henderson of Tyne Dock Youth Club. The clock was won by Thomas in the Frankie Vaughan Talent Competition of 1957.

Tommy Duffy receiving the winner's cup in the *What Makes A Star* competition at the Pier Pavilion. The presentation was made by one of the judges, Leslie Gould. The ranking for the evening was 1. Tommy Duffy, singer. 2. Sheila Giles, singer. 3. Bob Hedly, comedian. 4. Clive Ahmed, singer. 5. The Satellites, skiffle group. 6 Gordon Jones, singer.

Tom Best on South Shields Promenade, 1948. Tom was born in Florence Street but lived for many years in John Williams Street and attended Stanhope Road School from 1932. After leaving school he worked from the age of sixteen for T.L. Ainsley, a firm of nautical opticians and compass adjusters based at the Mill Dam, serving his time as a compass adjuster. His apprenticeship was interrupted when he was called up for the army at the age of eighteen in 1945. While in the army he served abroad in several European countries until 1948 when he rejoined civilian life and returned to his native town. Then he rejoined Ainsley's and finished his apprenticeship. Although his work brought him into contact with a great number of townspeople, he is perhaps better known, both locally and in the region, as an entertainer. He recalls:

'I first started in the entertainment business in the 1950s at the Unionist Club in Frederick Street. I was singing Nat King Cole and Perry Como songs – all the ballads. Then I managed to get myself into concert parties. On Sunday afternoons at 12.30 we would get up and sing until about two o'clock. There was no bingo on then, thank goodness. Often, when we had finished, the club concert secretaries, Arthur and Dickey Bell, would tell us that there had been a telephone call from a club in Newcastle, maybe the Union Jack Club, and they wanted two or three people from Shields that night. I would always have to ask my wife first but she would always say "alright love" and come along with me. With a few other artists we would get the bus to Newcastle from Chichester and were paid about thirty bob each.

I've always liked dancing. I went to the Crown Dance Hall in Ocean Road and the Hedworth Hall at Westoe where there were some real characters. There was Tom 'Tot' Wright, a marvellous dancer and a singer, who was quite good looking but was never seen without his big wellies. They were big and heavy and turned over at the top. None of the girls refused a dance with him because he was such a marvellous dancer. Through the day he would push a two wheeled cart around the town with bits of scrap like a rag and bone man still wearing the same wellies.'

Puppeteer Tom Finch, with Fred and Margaret, his son and daughter. After leaving the army in 1945 Tom Finch formed a group of puppeteers with friends and neighbours. The group disbanded around a year later and Tom was left on his own. He carried on with his wife and members of his own family, calling the performing group 'The Tom and Emma Finch Marionettes'. Tom made the stage and the family operated the curtains and lights. They have been performing in Shields ever since. *Below*: Tom and Emma Finch's invitation to appear on the popular TV talent show, *Opportunity Knocks*.

Thames Television

Thames Television Limited
Teddington Lock
Teddington
Middlesex
* 01-977 3252   ext. 512

30 June 1969

Mr. and Mrs T. Finch
213 Bamburgh Avenue,
South Shields,
Northumberland.

Dear Mr. and Mrs Finch,

I would be pleased if you would telephone me reverse charges on the above number as soon as possible to advise me as to whether you would be free on 19th and 20th August should we be able to offer you an engagement on our programme OPPORTUNITY KNOCKS on those dates.

Yours sincerely,

Barbara Faulkner
Casting

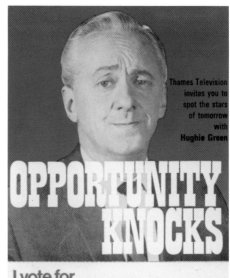

Thames Television invites you to spot the stars of tomorrow with **Hughie Green**

OPPORTUNITY KNOCKS

I vote for

During the 1950s and '60s, Shields' artist Tom Finch was the head of the Art Department at Joplings' store in Sunderland. Amongst his other work he produced these psychedelic designs for an in-store fashion show.

Harton Colliery Band on tour in the early 1930s. Included are:
Denis Scoins (principal cornet) Fred Atherton (Eb bass and band secretary) and Bob Smith (solo euphonium). They were recognized as one of the finest bands this country has produced.

The St Hilda Colliery Band.

The following article about the successes of the band was written by band member Sgt J.G. Oliver in the 1960s:

'At about 9 pm, news arrived in South Shields that in a matter of minutes electrified the town. Scenes of jubilant and enthusiastic crowds seldom ever seen before in the County Borough of South Shields greeted the news that St Hilda Colliery Band had won the One Thousand Guineas Challenge Trophy and Championship Brass Band Contest at Crystal Palace.

They had worked and planned through years of hard work to win this coverted trophy. These ideas began to bear fruit in the early part of this century, under the guidance of that great organiser Mr John Trelease. In September 1908 the band won the Junior Cup at Crystal Palace. In 1909 the band won the Grand Shield, the stepping stone to the Championship Contest.

When the trophy was won on the day of 26th September 1912 the scenes of elation were only surpassed by those the following Tuesday night when the champion band arrived at South Shields Railway Station and were escorted to the Town Hall forecourt and given a civic reception.

Then came 1913. The men were in no doubts as to what was expected of them. They had learned how to get to the top. Now they experienced how hard it is to keep there. The result of the 1913 Championship was Irwell Springs Band – 1st, St Hilda Colliery Band – 2nd.

Then alas came the First World War and most of the young members joined the forces. The band was carried on most effectively by many older bandsmen of the town and let it be said to their great credit raised a sum during the war for charities of about £13,000. Then came the Armistice and the return of members from the forces.

From now on we have the great combination of one of the greatest of all band managers, Mr James Southern, and bandmaster, the late Mr James Oliver, who made a great success of providing programme music to suit all tastes. This famous pair were to see further championship successes in 1920, 1921, 1924 and 1926 and also a Command Performance before their Majesties the King and Queen at Buckingham Palace.

There were also extended tours throughout Great Britain and Ireland, followed by that great and never to be forgotten tour of Canada where Tynesiders travelled hundreds of miles to renew Auld Acquaintance.

Having talked so much about this great band let us not forget the other great bands we have with us: Marsden Colliery Band who won the Crystal Palace Championship and One Thousand Guineas Trophy in 1925. The Harton Colliery Band which apart from winning Belle Vue Manchester Open Championship contest in 1919 had gone so very near to winning the Crystal Palace Championship. This band has proved itself one of our finest concert bands and now one would say 'Carry on the good work Harton'.

Now may I mention a band where a boy can be thoroughly taught and provided with an instrument, clothing and given a chance to start on a musical career second to none. The band of the 1st Cadet Battalion (The Durham Light Infantry) Londonderry Hall, South Shields.'

The St Hilda Colliery Band pictured in 1922 preparing to cross to the Isle of Wight for engagements at Shanklin and Ryde. The band are travelling in their then state-of-the-art Leyland touring bus complete with solid tyres. This was a self-contained vehicle which carried the band members and all equipment during their most extensive nation-wide summer tours.

Pictured in a Brighton chalet while on tour in the late 1920s are, from left to right: George Oliver (cornetist and pianist) James Southern (manager and owner of the band) and James Oliver (musical director). In 1929 the band became the St Hilda Professional Band – the only professional brass band in this country to have existed.

A tea break for thirsty bandsmen. They are pictured in their scarlet, royal blue and gold uniforms specially made for the bands' annual six weeks Christmas engagement at Bertram Mills, London Olympia Circus, 1927-33.

A poster for the Town Summer
Carnival, 1927.

A local girl in costume for one of
the town's summer carnivals.

Members of Hospital Radio South Tyneside taking part in the town's annual
parade from the new Town Hall to the flower show in the Bents Park. Some of
the members are dressed as Robinson's Jam Gollywogs while others are
wearing 'Scotsman' outfits.

Three publicity photographs of local performer Thomas Dodds Johns and entourage taken in the studios of the Speed Photography Company, Ocean Road. He was born in Mortimer Road in 1907 and began his career in Shields at the Queen's and Alexandra Theatres. Later he travelled the UK in such big shows as *Bless the Bride* and *The Student Prince*. Many of the terms in his contracts make interesting reading: 'The Manager shall provide the necessary dresses for the various roles the artist shall be called upon to sustain, and the artist shall provide all wigs, tights, stockings, sandals, boots, shoes, feathers, ornaments and all under garments which are to be of good quality and to be reasonably approved by the manager. Acts of familiarity between ladies and gentleman of the company, or local stage staff, or any unseemly conduct, abusive or insulting language, will not be tolerated. Ladies and Gentlemen must not under any circumstances live at the same address.'

Hospital Radio South Tyneside member Gerry Jenkins receiving an award for his long service to the station from Chairwoman Eleanor Minikin, *circa* 1983. The occasion, the new studios at South Tyneside General Hospital were officially opened by television presenter Bill Steele. They were situated in a room at the side of the Hospital Chapel. The station had previously occupied a room in the Ingham Infirmary, the building is now part of the residential development, Ingham Grange. With the massive rebuilding on the General Hospital site the Chapel has since been demolished and the station has moved to purpose-built studios in the new Ingham Wing.

Chairman of Hospital Radio South Tyneside, Ian Wilkinson, under the railway bridge in King Street during a fundraising road show for the radio station. Ian was a colliery mechanic by profession and a member of the Salvation Army as well as chairman of HRST for several years. The authors believe he currently lives in Iceland where he is a school band instructor. Occasionally he returns to Shields. Hospital Radio began with Radio Trinity House using equipment donated by Rediffusion. Notable names involved included Ron Drew and John Tyzack. In 1969 Radio Shields was registered as a company by a group of local businessmen including Charles Dallas, former Conservative parliamentary candidate for the town, Sir Robert Chapman, and Mr J. Ireland, newsagent. Although there have been several restricted service license stations, including Seven FM, a full-time service for the town has yet to materialize.

SECTION FIVE

SPECIAL MOMENTS

The Harbour ... The Fair ... In The Park ... Special Occasions And Special Visits ... Boating ... Just Out Walking ...

A quiet moment on the pier. This and some of the other photographs in this chapter were taken by local photographer Ron Bell in the 1980s as part of a study of the area around the harbour and pier.

This looks like a rowing gala in the harbour with what appears to be a crew from one boat clambering back inside fully clothed and soaking wet. At first sight some appear to be women, however on second glance they may all be men in fancy dress. This may have

been a mock battle. The poles being wielded may be paddles, or as one bears the legend 'AS', they may be some kind of indicators. The boat seems to have a funnel. Perhaps the engine has failed and the boat is in danger of being swept out to sea explaining why a line has been attached and the improvised paddles.

South Shields Skating Rink, 1910.

A group of Shields' people picnicking behind the Beach Cafe on the foreshore, 1927.

Three images taken around the North Foreshore by photographer Ron Bell in the 1970s.

Sheila Bruce with her cousins Billy, Leslie, Charlie and Duncan on the pier. The date is likely to be 1938 and the carefree looking child staring through the telescope is an ominous foreshadowing of events to come. In what would likely be a matter of months the pier would be sealed off and would not re-open to the public until after the Second World War.

Sheila Bruce with one of her cousins outside their beach tent. In comparison with today they both appear quite 'dressed', reflecting that for many, time on the beach could almost be a formal occasion.

One of the now demolished confectionery stalls opposite the pier head, *circa* 1978.

The bride and groom and members of a wedding party, whose reception was taking place at the Sea Hotel, pause for a moment outside one of the area's many fish and chip stalls.

Above and right: Attractions in the Ocean Beach Pleasure Park.

Below: Billy Lamb aged six and his uncle William Laing on the fairground's 'Galloping Horses' in 1951.

Breaking the ice on the North Marine Park.

A trolley bus picks up passengers on the South Foreshore. This area has seen much holiday development since the Second World War including extensions of the promenade south, Gypsies Green stadium and Italian style fountains.

One of the signs that the Second World War was really over was the resumption of pleasure boat trips. Ex-Royal Navy Officer Leo Earle bought several ex-Army amphibious landing craft (DUKWs) and gave trips around the harbour during the Summer season. Here he is seen inside the craft on what was probably a test run in early 1948 from the little beach, with Motor Boat Club colleague, close friend and DUKW mechanic Harry Wray.

The South Shields' Motor Boat and Yacht Club at River Drive in 1957. The club was founded in 1946. Club Secretary Harry Wray's houseboat *Good Intent* can be seen at the rear to the left by the clubhouse. To the right is Jack Swinburn's boat building yard.

The Mill on Cleadon Hills. This is a favourite area to walk and exercise dogs.

Ernie Branch at Cleadon Hills looking towards the South Pier, *circa* 1927. Being quite easily reached by electric tram from the town, this area became a popular spot for picnicking once the Cleadon Light Railway was opened in late 1922.

Cleadon Hills, 1927.

GREAT SCHEMES AND UNFULFILLED DREAMS

*The Pendulum And The Pit ... A Transporter Bridge ... Shipley's
Drop From The Clouds ... Electricity Works and Tramways ... The
Shining Blue Wonders ... New Dawns Fade ...*

In the nineteenth century the local powers that be ordered that many of the
railways into the town should be built on embankments to avoid blocking
thoroughfares such as King Street with level crossings. However, this tended to
block off parts of the town, with builders often skimping on bridges. Here in
1903 the former Smith Street tunnel near High Shields is being replaced by a
much wider metal frame bridge. Once the new structure is secure the old
tunnel will be dug out and removed.

The Pendulum And The Pit

A drawing of the experimental pendulum room at the bottom of Harton Colliery used in September and October 1854 by Professor Airey, the Astronomer Royal, as part of his apparatus to determine the weight of the Earth. At that time Harton was 1,260 feet deep with underground passages of more than 100 miles in extent. The apparatus used consisted of two astronomical clocks and two invariable Kater's pendulums suspended on a knife edge of very hard steel.

One clock and one pendulum were located at ground level, the other inside the specially built pendulum room shown. Regular observations were taken from a barometer and a thermometer fixed at each station so corrections for temperature and atmospheric pressure could also be made. As far as the authors understand it, Airey theorised that gravitational force is higher underground because the Earth is denser, meaning an underground pendulum would swing faster than one above. Using an electrical signal to synchronise each clock, the number of swings made by each pendulum every four hours was noted and the process repeated many times over four days. Then the pendulums swapped over to reduce error and the whole process repeated again. By comparison of the difference between each number of swings and then with the distance between the pendulums Airey could calculate the weight of the earth between them and then through extrapolation the weight of the entire Earth. Airey concluded that the Earth had a weight of 6,000,000,000,000,000,000,000 tons. The authors are not clear if Airey was indeed measuring the weight of the earth or its mass, as a body travelling freely in space does not have weight as such. Even after much discussion and consultation with the regulars of the Old Ship Inn, we are still unsure on this point.

A Transporter Bridge

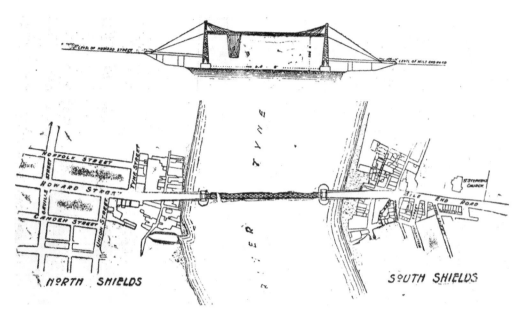

Anyone climbing up the bank from the North Shields ferry landing stage will see the stub like end of street above them to their right, looking like it was made to be the approach to a cross Tyne bridge. On 23rd February 1825 a 'numerous and highly respectable' meeting of the inhabitants of North and South Shields was held at the Northumberland Arms, New Quay, North Shields to consider a scheme proposed by a Captain Brown of the Royal Navy. He proposed a suspension bridge to connect the two boroughs at a very high elevation: 'Sufficiently above the water to admit ships to sail thereunder without striking their masts, starting near the library at North Shields and near the north end of Westoe Lane, South Shields. The cost of this undertaking was variously estimated at from £93,000 to £150,000. The proposal illustrated above dates from the late 1800s and would have involve the construction of a type of ferry bridge that was finding favour on the continent at that time. The proposed height of the bridge above the high water mark would have been 200 ft. A contemporary article described it as having a platform: 'To support the special form of car designed for the transportation of passengers' carts and vehicles of all kinds. Four lines of rails are laid down, upon which run sixty small wheels in pairs. To these wheels are fixed thirty steel vertical cables which are fastened to the car. The car is eleven metres in length, and thirteen metres broad. The central platform is meant for vehicles and can accommodate a number of carts, horse riders and cyclists. On each side are spaces intended for foot passengers; the right side is covered in and reserved for first class pedestrians. That on the left is protected by an awning and intended for commoner folk.' The idea lingered on until the 1950s before the Tyne Tunnel finally laid it to rest. To clear the Tyne properly a bridge would likely involved a combination of steep gradients and wholesale demolition on the South Shields side, with the road coming down to Earth on Mile End Road somewhere near the Station Taxies office. However, only recently a somewhat fantastic scheme to link the North and South piers by a bridge between each lighthouse was discussed in the local press.

Shipley's drop Frae The Cloods

What must have been one of the first parachute jumps on Tyneside was staged from Westoe Cricket Field on Saturday, 5th April 1890. The aeronaut in question was a Mr W.H. Shipley of John Clay Street, a painter who according to his neighbours had never before been higher than a two storey ladder. According to a contemporary account, Mr Shipley's voyage began from Westoe Village:

'A large space of ground adjoining the Westoe Cricket Field, and fronting Meldon Terrace and enclosed by canvass paling seven feet high. Within this the monster balloon lay, and early in the afternoon commenced filling with gas from the South Shields Gas Company. By half past four an enormous crowd had assembled to watch the preparations. The West Dock Band was in attendance and dispensed several lively airs while the preliminaries were being completed. At five o'clock Mr Shipley arrived, dressed in a dark velvet costume, and was loudly cheered as he entered the enclosure. At twenty minutes past five the balloon ascended, drifting towards the Tyne. When it had reached an altitude of 9,000 feet, Mr Shipley detached himself. He eventually came down on the top of 51 and 53 John Williamson Street, witnessed by thousands of people on both sides of the lower Tyne. A large excited crowd soon gathered in the street as he slid down an outhouse and got into an open carriage that was on the spot ready for him. The driver had great difficulty making progress through the crowd, which was augmenting every moment by people anxious to shake hands with Mr Shipley. They were only a short distance up Laygate Lane when his admirers unyoked the horses and began pushing the carriage themselves. Thus they proceeded amidst tumultuous cheering till reaching the foot of Westoe Village, when Mr Flemming, a very powerful man, got the aeronaut on his shoulders and carried him around the road skirting the Westoe Cricket Field, past Woods Terrace and there into the enclosed space from which the ascent had been made. A few words were addressed to the assemblage in the field, and then Mr Flemming trotted off again with the hero of the hour to Mr Samuel Harvey's house in Meldon Terrace. Apparently that weekend there were comments made that the accent could have been higher and Mr Shipley decided to make another jump the following Monday. Monday was a day of heavy showers and it wasn't until ten minutes to six that the balloon took off again from Westoe Cricket Ground.

The balloon shot up swiftly and in less than three minutes it had passed far beyond the altitude reached on Saturday and was still going skywards at a rapid rate when the daring amateur detached himself. The atmosphere was extremely clear; the balloon being very distinctly outlined against the almost cloudless sky. For a moment only a speck was seen below it, and then the parachute expanded. It appeared like a huge mushroom in the distance. Gradually descending it moved before the breeze and passed over a great number of fields covering possibly two miles of ground before alighting in a field close to a farm some distance beyond Cleadon Village. After arriving back at Meldon Terrace, Shipley informed the crowd that he had reached a height of 15,000 ft and that the view of the country he had up aloft was magnificent. He could not distinguish a single sound except the beating of the waves and he thought at one time he was going to land somewhere near Marsden Rock. He expressed the hope that the persons who had been carping about the comparatively slight altitude he had previously reached, would now feel satisfied.'

Below is an abridged version of a poem describing Shipley's drop. For this truncation, the authors apologise to the original poet whose name we were unable to discover.

Noo had on, mee hinnies, and whisht till aw tell ye,
Hoo Shipley hes proved hissel fairly a man,
He up wiv his brushes and heavenwards rushes,
And Leaves us awl gyepen as hard as we can:
Sum carled him a hero, and sum a great ass,
Sum said wi'poor Shipley it's awl up a tree,
Says he noo awl show them it isn't awl gas,
Awl soon let them see what a painter can dee.

Hurrah to wor rockets, hurrah to wor lifeboats,
Hurrah to wor gud-temperd star-gazin croods,
Hurrah to wor Shipley, wor own painter Shipley,
Hurrah to wor Shipley that dropped from the cloods

The day wis fixed on, the balloon wis myde up,
And sum said the painter wid funk at the last,
But Shipley he knew them, and swore he wid jew them,
And wadn't back oot whin his word wis once passed.

An mercy on me what a swarm did aw see,
There wus millions of drapers and watchmakers there,
An aw thought to mesel as aw wanderd alang,
An saw every face wis in wonderment filled.
Hoo larnin's advancing wi scheull-boards an dancing –
For wi awl half expected a man to be killed.

But a pitman like me very far cannot see,
So aw mixed in the crowd with the cuffs and the lace;
An watched some gay foxes just dodging the boxes
To pay for the show wi they hadn't the grace.
There was Sal wi the lodger, an Bessie wi Roger,
An two reet in front aw thought far ower kind,
There was Robert wi Mary that's often contrary
An a couple was bilin and cooing behind.

They made us feel sick, so aw wished he'd be quick,
An flee up above for the time was long passed;
But soon all wor eyes wor turned up to the skies,
An patience itsel wis rewarded at last,
Brave Shipley wis there rising high in the air.

How folkes opened their eyes when they saw the thing rise
An Shipley flee thousands o' feet in the air,
They shooted 'good-byes' and blinked with their eyes,
They'd made up their minds they wid see him nee mair,
But Shipley went up like a lark on the wing
An when he wis far enough, dropped like a stone,
Then the strong parachute like a sail opened oot,
An he said it was nice and would go up again.

South Shields Corporation Electricity Works

King Street, 1896. Electric arc lighting is installed although the gas lamps have not yet been removed. An industrial journal covered the introduction of electric power to South Shields:

'The opening of the municipal electricity works on the first of September marks an important step forwards in the development of the town. It is just seventy years ago that the gas lamps in South Shields were lighted for the first time: and the contrast between gas in 1826 introduced by a company, and electric light in 1896, introduced by the Corporation, is an instructive example of the changes that time inevitably brings.

The Corporation of South Shields is the first Local Authority on the Tyne to erect its own electricity works, and is certainly to be congratulated in that it has not allowed the supply of electrical energy to fall into the hands of a company. There would indeed have been little excuse for the city fathers of South Shields had they failed to profit by the example of the neighbouring town of Newcastle, where two electric lighting companies have been allowed to divide the rich spoils between them. With the exception of Sunderland, South Shields is the only town in the busy and populous North East coast district where the Corporation has undertaken the supply of electricity.

For the genesis of the scheme it is necessary to go back to 1893, in which year the Corporation obtained a report about the lighting of the borough. On the receipt of this report an Electric Light Committee was formed, and the members determined to appoint a borough electrical engineer, who should design the whole system and draw up all specifications. They were fortunate in obtaining the services of Mr Joseph A. Jeckell. From the first, Mr Jeckell determined that the tenders to be accepted should be those which offered the best value for the money, not just the lowest, it being his intention to have the best plant obtainable.

The power station is in the centre of the borough, and has a river

The engine house, South Shields Corporation electricity works.

frontage on the Tyne. The buildings are both spacious and well adapted for their purpose. The engineer's office opens direct on to a gallery in the engine room. There are two boilers of the ordinary marine type, their length being 10 feet 6 inches and diameter 11 feet. Each is capable of evaporating 5,000 lbs of water per hour with fair Northumberland steam coal. The bunkers are situated at the quay wall, so that the coal can be brought alongside and hoisted direct into them. The bunker doors are opposite the boilers, and thus the least possible labour is expended. The switchboard is a solid structure built into the wall. To avoid the proximity of wood, the platform is of stone and concrete. In the construction of the rectifier switchboard, which is placed between the two rectifiers, no wood has been used, slate and iron taking its place.

In the streets, arc lamp posts are of the 'gibbet' type and there are two small brackets on each, each bracket carrying two 16-candle power glow lamps. The posts are about sixty yards apart. Current will be charged for on the Brighton system, 6d for the first two hours of maximum demand and 3d for the rest. The price for heating purposes has been fixed at 3d, and for motive power at 2d.

At its meeting yesterday week, the council unanimously voted to at once extend the street lighting to Ocean Road and Fowler Street. A further extension to the High Shields district would also have been put on hand, but for the reason that the present season of the year is most unfavourable for the street opening operations. Next year, however, this work will certainly be carried out, the council having come to a clear understanding on the point.

These early decisions to extend speak hopefully for the future, and go to show that the South Shields Corporation does not intend to do things by halves. May this spirit long prevail and may South Shields prove a shining example of municipal electric lighting enterprise to its numerous neighbours on Tyneside, who appear to have the bump of cautiousness even more strongly developed than is usual near the border.'

The Corporation Electricity Works seems to have had a relatively quiet but prosperous life. Around 1906 there was some disquiet when Harton Coal Company engineers informed the Corporation Electricity Committee that they would be looking outside the town to the County of Durham Electrical Power Distribution Company for their energy. The Holborn station could only supply continuous current while the HCC wanted alternating current. The process of instilling the necessary heavy cabling through the streets to Hebburn for the HHC is unlikely to have pleased the Corporation either.

Left: This series of images apparently show the shut down and the beginning of dismantling, although the information that came with them is incomplete. The top photograph shows Messrs McArdle and Waugh switching off the rotary converter.

Over and underground: An electricity substation in Imeary Street used to convert voltage down from 2000V to 220V for domestic consumption. Amongst others, similar underground stations existed in Ocean Road, opposite the Royal Hotel, and Ogle Terrace and others for the tram and trolleybus systems. It would be interesting to know what still exists below Shields' streets.

South Shields Corporation Electric Tramways, 1906-46

Removal of road sets for the construction of the electric tram system. Possibly this is Eldon Street. South Shields Corporation went to Parliament for powers to build the electric system in 1901. However, amongst the townspeople there was strong feeling against the municipalisation of the tramways and on 8th January 1902 the idea was thrown out, 5,942 to 5,716 against by a statutory meeting of ratepayers. It took a promise that the operation of the system could be put out to private tender for the ratepayers to agree with a second attempt. On 30th March 1906 the first section opened between the corner of Fowler Street and Ocean Road to Stanhope Road with a line branching at right angles from Chichester through Laygate Lane to Adelaide Street. The track was also complete between Frederick Street/Reed Street and South Eldon Street but the need to demolish a block of property on Frederick Street corner meant there was a delay in the opening of that section. The whole system of a figure eight snaking across the town was operational by March 1907. Once complete, other than the Green Lane district there was hardly a place in the borough more than five minutes walk from a car stop.

VOTE FOR SPENCER.

(WITH APOLOGIES TO RUDYARD KIPLING).

He's a present-minded beggar, and his qualities are great,
   Shields Ward will take SPENCER as they find him,
He's full of active service and he'll keep down the rates,
   But no good thing will he leave behind him.

A True Son—A Shields' Son. Work for him with might.
   Electors Vote for him and don't forget—TO-DAY.
ELECTRIC TRAMS are wanted, for them he'll vote all right,
   Send SPENCER to the Council, he'll be sure to win
      his way.

Of course he will, he's just the man to do it.

Printed and Published by Jennings & Son, 22, Smithy Street, South Shields.

Left: A pamphlet for a Council Election in praise of trams. Electrification of the network was a political issue in the town.

Laying tram rails across Chichester. Even though this is one of the town's main junctions it's noticeable that the entire road is given over to construction work. It would be interesting to know what other road users felt about this.

The South Shields Corporation Tram Depot, Dean Road shortly before the system began operations. Originally tramcars can be seen as an expression of the 'class system'. Even on municipal networks, services often would not start until the working man was at work and then charged fares usually beyond their reach. It took until almost the outbreak of the First World War, and government pressure for the introduction of working man's penny returns, for the trams to be used by everyone. In the 1920s the situation was almost inverted, trams were used to open up the new Cleadon Park estate that re-housed many people from the less well-off areas. Private housing developments around Harton ensured the Cleadon Light Railway had the monopoly on the newer, faster cars. A Cleadon Lunch Express service allowed white collar workers to have lunch at home and be back at work within the hour.

Around 1930, the electric tramway is showing signs of maturity. This is the forecourt of the second Dean Road shed, now enclosed as part of the bus depot. The car in front is still in original condition, but is now layered with grime. It is attached to the other by a chain suggesting it may have been relegated to works use rather than, as local folklore suggests, being a car reserved for the residents of Tyne Dock.

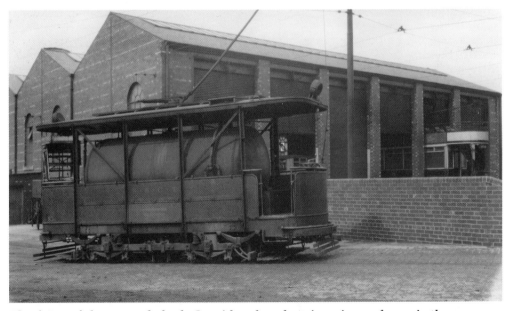

The front of the second shed. Outside, also showing signs of use, is the Corporation's water car. Bought in 1913 from the Brush Electrical Engineering Company, this 2,000 gallon water tank on wheels sprayed the streets with pressurised jets and was reputedly of great benefit in clearing the roads of horse droppings on hot summer days.

Works car No 3 was another of the tramways' backroom boys. Again it started life as a pristine open topper, but was cut down to a single deck works and snow plough car in 1934. Decorated with flags, ivy and spring flowers, its top deck packed with bowler hatted councillors, it is the same car that appears in the often reprinted souvenir photograph of 30th March 1906 (the opening of the first section of track).

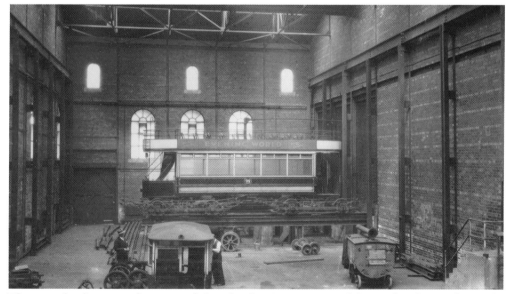

The repair shops at the rear of the sheds. Trams passed from the depot through the roll down doors to the right. The car shown here may be one of two bought from the Jarrow system on its closure in 1929. In the foreground, an old bus body appears to be being used as a stores or tea cabin.

The Shining Blue Wonders

A Corporation trolleybus on Marsden Lane in 1954. Driven by the Mayor, the first trolleybus service left the Market Place on 12th October 1936, running via Mortimer Road to Marsden Grotto. The scheme had been adopted by the Town Council in 1934, accepted by ratepayers later in the year and given the Royal Assent in August 1935. The first trolleybus was delivered on 14th September 1936 and test runs began almost immediately. On one such journey a reporter from the *Shields Gazette's, A Shields' Woman's Diary*, was on board:

'I rang Mr Muscroft, South Shields Transport Manager and said, "Please may I have a ride on a trolleybus." He said: yes, so I enjoy the distinction of being the first Shields' woman to ride round the town on one of these, the newest and most luxurious of our transport arrangements. I felt terrifically important, like the Duchess of York or somebody. For one afternoon I had my own private trolleybus complete with driver, trolley boy and Mr Crawford to 'do the honours' and show me the sights. Inside it is extremely luxurious and comfortable. Mr Crawford and I tried both downstairs and upstairs and I liked the upstairs best – it's lighter and you get a better view.

We swung smoothly down to the Market Place, round it and then back again and out to Cleadon leaving the tramway track at Stanhope Road. With no sound other than the strangely exciting swish, swish of the trolley poles sweeping along the overhead wires, we slid down the magnificent flower bordered new road to Marsden, under the new bridge there and so round the Mulberry bush (metaphorical: not planted yet) and back again to the tramway office.

I don't know if it's a peculiarity of Shields people or not, but they do look stupid when they are interested. Our trolleybus attracted a good deal of attention on this trial trip. People stopped and turned around to stare as the shining blue wonder swept passed them and they all looked blank as sheets of paper before you begin to write on them.

All except for Miss Florence Roberts, whom we passed at Cleadon. She really did look alert and interested until she saw me sitting inside and then even her mouth dropped open in a gape (sorry Miss Roberts and all that).'

Trolleybus, No 213, arrives at Westoe. This was a batch of around fourteen vehicles which arrived in the town during 1937 and unlike the earlier buses these were direct replacements for the tramcars. The license for No 213 is recorded as being 'revoked' in 1963 as the system was winding down. The bus was undoubtedly scrapped, its exact fate is unclear.

Trolleybuses parked in the former tram sheds. Although not featuring in official guide books this scene is arguably one the classic views of Shields. Ironically the vestiges of the tram tracks were to far outlast the trolleybuses, some still remain inside the depot.

In 1959 alterations to the Dean Road depot caused the town's fifty strong trolleybus fleet to be parked along King George Road at night. Although a formal closure declaration was not made by the transport committee until the end of that year, the fact that they were all expelled from the depot while the motor buses were kept safely inside was an obvious omen of things to come.

Redundant trolleybuses parked at the side of the depot in 1964. Closure became official policy on the 19th September 1959, although a stay of execution was announced shortly afterwards. However, proposals to gradually move traffic out of King Street in favour of the new Kepple Street would have meant new overhead would be needed for the system to continue, and this was judged as just too expensive. While the first official bus, No 200, had been cheered on by crowds in the Market Place, closure was a non event. New motor buses were gradually brought in until on the morning of 30th April 1964 the overhead was simply not switched on. One trolleybus went into preservation, and some electrical equipment was bought by the NCB.

New Dawns Fade

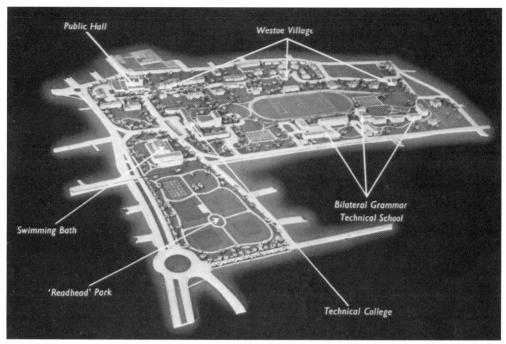

After the damage caused to the town by the Second World War, much thought went into the possibilities offered by reconstruction. Pictured are outlines for the redevelopment of the seafront and Westoe areas. Fortunately or unfortunately, these proposals were never developed directly, although some of the ideas expressed here have resurfaced throughout the last five decades.

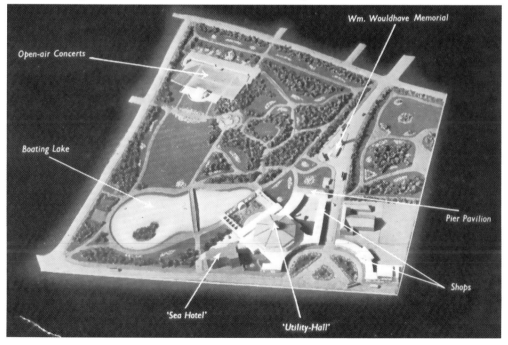

Acknowledgements

The authors would like to thank the following people who have lent us stories and/or photographs and otherwise actively assisted with the production of this book:

Eddie Angel, Geordie Atkinson, Keith Bardwell, Ron Bell, Tom Best, Dennis Boad, Colin G. Branch, Ernie Branch, David H. Branch, Isabelle Branch, Sue Branch, Violet Branch, Zoe Branch, Kathleen Burdon, Ken Courner, David Charlton, Andrew Clark, Ron Davison, Thomas John Dodds, Tommy Duffy (Alan Fox), Emma Finch, Tom Finch, Mary Gibbs, John Gordon, Malcolm Grady, Muriel Hanson, Frank Heywood, Shirley Mei Jung Huang, Mr and Mrs Ken Johnson, Doris Johnson, Joan Mullen, Margaret Pickering, Eddie Post, George Post, Joyce Roberts, J.W. Bone, Flo Thorburn, Ken Tully and members of Northumbria Police, Mary McNeeny, Cuthbert Nicholson, Kathleen Nicholson, Alan Packer, Dallas Park, John Rutherford, Irene Spence, Stuart Smith, Thelma Small (née Taws), Marjorie Summers, Sheila Tweddell, Stan Tweddell, Robert Wray, Mark Walsh and Stan Walsh. Additional thanks to past and present members of St Lawrence's Church. South Shields Grammar School/Harton Comprehensive/ Harton School, Laygate Lane School, St Gregory's Church, St Peter's Church, St Hilda's Church, Westoe Methodist Church and everyone at the Victorian South Shields class.

Additionally thanks are due to Dennis Boad, Robert Wray and Lisa Whiteley for additional research and proof reading. Finally we would like to thank the unnamed and untraceable writers of articles about the town from which we have drawn much of the written material for this book. We hope their prose style hasn't been too butchered in our efforts to fit their words around someone else's pictures.

Photos, courtesy of:

South Tyneside Libraries 1 19b 21b 39 48t 49t 53t 56b 58t 111 121t

Mr David Packer 5 11t 14t 41t 49b 51t 53bl 108b

The Shields Gazette 6 40t 42b 47t 71 75 77 86 92 94t 127

National Tramway Museum Back Cover
National Tramway Museum/Geoff Cunningham 7
National Tramway Museum/ H. Nicol 61t 121 123b
National Tramway Museum/ Camwell 123t

Newcastle Libraries 30t 54 102

Beamish The North Of England Open Air Museum 8b 17t 19 22 47t 54t 56t 121b

The K Hoyle Rail Study Centre North Road Darlington centre 26 38 40 52t

Front cover: From left to right: Rita Hill, Pamela Hutchins and Margaret Stewart in the garden of 48 Morpeth Avenue. Margaret Stewart went on to own Stewart's newsagents in Harton Village.

Back cover: Fowler Street, *circa* 1935.